What Lies Before Us

What Lies Before Us

Morris Panych

Talonbooks
Vancouver

Talonbooks
P.O. Box 2076, Vancouver, British Columbia, Canada V6B 3S3
www.talonbooks.com

Typeset in New Baskerville and printed and bound in Canada.

First Printing: 2007

The publisher gratefully acknowledges the financial support of the Canada Council for the Arts; the Government of Canada through the Book Publishing Industry Development Program; and the Province of British Columbia through the British Columbia Arts Council and the Book Publishing Tax Credit for our publishing activities.

Library and Archives Canada Cataloguing in Publication

Panych, Morris
    What lies before us / Morris Panych.

A play.
ISBN 978-0-88922-560-2

    I. Title.

PS8581.A65W43 2007   C812'.54   C2006-905729-X

The world premiere of *What Lies Before Us* was presented by CanStage, in a Crow's Theatre production, on January 18, 2007 in Toronto, with the following cast and crew:

AMBROSE .... David Storch
KEATING .... Matthew MacFadzean
WING .... Wayne Sujo

Director: Jim Millan
Producer: Gillian Hards, Crow's Theatre
Set & Costume Design: Ken MacDonald
Lighting Design: Lesley Wilkinson
Sound Design & Original Music: John Gzowski
Stage Manager: Tanya Greve

Scene One

1885. A tent, hashed together out of bits of canvas; outside a late September wind blows, tugging a little at the canvas. MR. KEATING, a young assistant surveyor for the railroad, sitting on a crate, eating something chewy out of a tin; nearby AMBROSE, another assistant surveyor, watches with quiet disdain. Although they both wear suits and collars, KEATING's attire becomes more dishevelled as time goes on; and time does go on.

Mid-bite, KEATING notices AMBROSE.

KEATING
What?

AMBROSE
Nothing.

Unable to disengage.

Didn't you just eat?

KEATING keeps eating. AMBROSE goes back to making an entry in his journal. Finished his meal, KEATING begins sucking his teeth. AMBROSE stops, pen poised, looking directly forward; composing his thoughts.

AMBROSE
I realize we're in the middle of nowhere, but do you have to – do that?

KEATING

Do what?

AMBROSE

That.

KEATING

What? What do you want me to do?

AMBROSE

Perhaps you could refrain, if you would, from extracting bits of food from between your teeth, obstreperously, with screeds of wet suction? Or is that too much to ask?

KEATING

What's with you, lately?

AMBROSE

Lately?

KEATING

You're on my case day and night. Did you know that?

AMBROSE

Really.

KEATING

Lay off, Ambrose. A guy has to suck his teeth now and again. Next you'll be telling me not to scratch my own ass. What are you writing, now?

AMBROSE

None of your business.

KEATING

Well, maybe I don't like it. Maybe it offends my sensibilities.

AMBROSE

Sensibilities?

KEATING
You're not the only one with feelings.

AMBROSE
I can't imagine anything offending you.

KEATING
I have meat stuck in my teeth. What am I supposed to do?

AMBROSE
Try using some thread.

KEATING
Hey. Know what? Guess what, Ambrose. *I'm* going to start a journal.

AMBROSE
Go ahead.

KEATING
I might.

AMBROSE
Fine.

KEATING
Let's see. What'll I write about?

AMBROSE
Yes. That would be interesting. What does a man without a single thought in his head commit to his journal? The imagination reels.

KEATING
Thread?

AMBROSE
What?

KEATING
How do you get the meat out of your teeth with thread?

AMBROSE
How do you think?

KEATING thinks.

KEATING
Have you got any?

AMBROSE
No.

KEATING
Liar. It's in your kit.

AMBROSE
Then why did you ask?

KEATING
Just testing you.

AMBROSE
Use your own thread.

KEATING
Why would I have thread out here?

AMBROSE
What's happened to my – ?

AMBROSE moves his head about oddly, unable to focus; the glass is missing from one side of his spectacles.

KEATING
Would string work?

AMBROSE
No.

KEATING
   What about rope?

AMBROSE
   The idea, stupid, is to get it between your teeth, and
   then pull the meat out.

KEATING
   That doesn't work.

AMBROSE
   Must you disagree with me on absolutely every subject,
   Keating, even the ones you have absolutely no grasp
   of, whatsoever? Is it my lot in life to be continually
   upbraided by the world's most celebrated nitwit? I
   guess it just wasn't bad enough that I was stuck here
   on this misadventure with you and your out of tune
   guitar; wondering when, if ever, the Major would
   bother to show up. No; you have to share with me
   your every opinion as well.

KEATING
   It isn't an opinion. If you stick thread in, then it'll
   push the meat further into your teeth.

AMBROSE
   The thread gets behind the meat. It pulls the meat
   forward.

KEATING
   No it doesn't.

AMBROSE
   Something's happened to my vision.

KEATING
   That pen would work.

   Outside, a wolf howls. AMBROSE looks up.

   It's only a coyote.

AMBROSE
It's not a coyote.

KEATING
It is.

AMBROSE
It isn't.

KEATING
What makes you such an authority on everything,
Ambrose? I say it's a coyote. A wolf howls like this.

He howls.

AMBROSE
Yes, if it was crossed with a bloodhound, and had a
mouthful of walnuts.

KEATING
And just what are your educational qualifications, I'd
like to know.

AMBROSE
Let's see; I went to school for one.

KEATING
So did I.

AMBROSE
Right. What was the name of that college again?

KEATING
I didn't say it was a college.

AMBROSE
I believe you said it was a college.

KEATING
I don't believe so.

AMBROSE
  Yes; a college.

KEATING
  It was more of a seminary – really.

AMBROSE
  A seminary.

KEATING
  Why not?

AMBROSE
  First off, what could possibly have interested you in
  the priesthood, aside from the indiscriminate
  buggery?

KEATING
  I have my spiritual side. Only kidding.

AMBROSE
  Second, and more importantly, could somebody tell
  me what kind of engineering degree one gets from a
  seminary?

KEATING
  Who needs an engineering degree?

AMBROSE
  An engineer.

KEATING
  We're not engineers, Ambrose. We're surveyors. Not
  even surveyors. We're junior surveyors, might I
  remind you; lowly apprentices. You're overqualified;
  that's your problem. Overqualified.

  AMBROSE realizes the glass is missing.

AMBROSE
  My God. I thought I was going blind.

KEATING

What happened to that coolie?

AMBROSE

Did you sit on these?

KEATING

I want to have my bath. He never does what he's told.

AMBROSE

Well, you can't just shout at him in English, Keating.

KEATING

Why not?

AMBROSE

For one thing, he doesn't know English.

KEATING

Doesn't know English? Who doesn't know English?

AMBROSE

The non-English; for one.

KEATING

I could speak it when I was two.

AMBROSE

Somebody sat on these.

KEATING

Where is he?

AMBROSE

Go find him.

KEATING

Why don't you go find him? .

AMBROSE

Because I don't want him.

KEATING
What about a bath?

AMBROSE
I'm not having one.

KEATING
I want a bath.

AMBROSE
Stop whining, then. Go look for him. And try using his name; he might respond to that.

KEATING
What's his name again? Wong?

AMBROSE
Wing.

KEATING
Wing?

AMBROSE
Where is the goddamn glass? Is it not bad enough that I can't bear the sight of this place? Now I can't even see it.

KEATING
What a stupid name.

AMBROSE
What?

KEATING
Wing.

AMBROSE
I didn't name him.

KEATING

Imagine looking down at a cute little newborn, all
crumpled and pink and wide-eyed and thinking, I'm
going to name this dear sweet child after a flappy bird
part. What is going on over there in China?

AMBROSE

You could heat the water yourself.

KEATING

I don't know how.

AMBROSE

This is a nightmare.

*From now on, AMBROSE has to look at everything
askance to see it properly.*

KEATING

Now I'm going to have to wait. (*loudly*) Wing! Wing!

I feel like an idiot, shouting that name. To hell with
him. Stupid little twat. With any luck he's fallen into a
crevice.

AMBROSE

You'd better hope not. He's the only one who knows
how to start a fire.

KEATING

I can start a fire.

AMBROSE

You can't even put one out.

KEATING

If you'll excuse me, I'm going to continue with my
song.

AMBROSE

Oh, joy.

KEATING picks up a guitar and begins strumming, trying to write a song.

KEATING

Her name was Melinda. I saw her last night. She stood in the winda, beneath the moon – light. (*looking for a chord*) Moon – light. Moon – light.

AMBROSE

"Winda," by the way, is not a word.

KEATING

What?

AMBROSE

Here it is. What's it doing here?

KEATING

This is my song, Ambrose. My personal song. If it's all the same to you.

AMBROSE

Isn't Melinda the one who gave you syphilis?

KEATING

It's a romantic reinterpretation.

AMBROSE

How on earth did this come loose?

He tries to repair his spectacles, only to discover that, unable to do so, he must place the loose glass in his one eye, and wear the spectacles for the other.

KEATING

Everything I do, tonight, everything I say, you have a problem with.

AMBROSE

I have no problem with your song. I was just pointing out that, since you're so big on everyone speaking

English around here, you might like to know that "winda" is not a word.

KEATING

I know it's not a word! I am aware of that rather obvious boring fact! Songs don't use words, they use lyrics. I can't say "window" unless her name is "Melindow." So there goes your stupid theory.

AMBROSE

Perhaps, instead of the window, she could be standing in the *door*, then you could say she was a *whore*.

KEATING

Uh, yeah. That would be great, except for the fact she wasn't.

AMBROSE

Let me get this straight, then. You had your way with her, but you didn't give her any money.

KEATING

I gave her money, but it wasn't for that.

AMBROSE

No?

KEATING

It was as a gesture, if you must know. A parting gesture. And stop calling her a whore.

AMBROSE

Sorry. Professional dancer.

KEATING

You didn't see how high her legs went.

AMBROSE

No. And I didn't appreciate you making me wait in that – saloon either. Ever played poker with Mennonites?

KEATING

You won a Bible.

AMBROSE

Germans. Need I say more?

KEATING

Why didn't you fuck that big redhead in the black
dress like I told you.

AMBROSE

That was an Armenian monk.

KEATING

You set your standards too high, Ambrose.

AMBROSE

Do you ever listen to a word you say?

KEATING

What?

AMBROSE

Besides, I have a fiancée. As fate would have it.

KEATING

Fiancée? That can't be true.

AMBROSE

Yes, Keating. Believe it or not, somewhere back there,
some poor deluded young woman with slightly large
teeth waits for my return; folding into her diary a
wilted lily of the valley corsage and a program from
the Aberdeen Light Operatic Society's production of
The Bells of Corneville, from the latest of our many
tedious outings.

KEATING

To be honest, you don't seem like the marrying type,
if you know what I mean.

AMBROSE

I'm doing it for more honourable reasons than you can imagine, Keating. To piss my mother off. She has a thing about dental irregularities. Not to mention her distaste for the upper class.

KEATING

Aristocratic, is she; your fiancée?

AMBROSE

She has the breeding of a thoroughbred – and the looks to go with it.

KEATING

I don't get you, Ambrose. You're a mystery.

AMBROSE

Am I?

KEATING

May I be candid? Of course I may. What's missing in your life is God.

AMBROSE

Mine and everybody else's. Can't you sit still for a minute?

KEATING

I'm itchy. Not only that, you think too much. Why think about anything at all; that's my philosophy.

AMBROSE

Yes, you're right; as usual. Who cares if we're surrounded by the most dedicated and persistent of carnivores; mauled to death, eaten. Actually, wait a minute – I don't care, come to think of it. What difference does it make to me if I'm torn apart by an ill-tempered badger? I think carrion is a fitting end to the human experiment.

KEATING

It was a raccoon.

AMBROSE

It didn't look like a raccoon.

KEATING

Is that why you refuse to leave the tent?

AMBROSE

I don't refuse to leave the tent. I simply refuse to go out in the open air. And, oh by the way, that's another thing. I thought you had some familiarity with the wilderness. Isn't that what you told the Major? "Oh, don't worry about us. I have some familiarity with the wilderness." Tell me: aside from, say, a ramble through the blueberry patch, to have it off with some poor, unsuspecting member of the Middlesex Women's Lawn Bowling Association, what exactly is the source of this vast wilderness knowledge of yours?

KEATING

If you're going to be like that.

AMBROSE

Just curious.

KEATING

I've done some reading.

AMBROSE

Some reading.

KEATING

Coleridge.

AMBROSE

So if we run into an albatross –

KEATING

What's there to know about the wilderness? It's all completely straightforward and actually quite tedious. Certain berries are edible, for instance, certain berries aren't.

AMBROSE

If only you knew which.

KEATING

The red ones, obviously.

AMBROSE

I admire your blissful ignorance, Keating; really. But has it occurred to you, yet, that it's the end of September? It's already snowed, once. Snowed.

KEATING

A light dusting.

AMBROSE

Berries are beside the point. They should have been here by now. Quit – farting.

KEATING

I'll quit farting when you quit complaining about it.

AMBROSE

If you didn't eat everything in your path. That food might have to last us.

KEATING

We can always hunt for some.

AMBROSE

Hunt!?

KEATING

We've got a rifle.

AMBROSE
If only you hadn't used all the ammunition, shooting a rodent.

KEATING
Beaver.

AMBROSE
Exactly.

KEATING
I didn't like the inhospitable noise it was making. That was an inhospitable noise.

AMBROSE
It was inhospitable, I agree. But why not just kill it? Did you need to appliqué it to a tree?

KEATING
Got carried away.

AMBROSE
So what's the plan, now? Beat some poor creature to death with the gun barrel? You can forget hunting. We have exactly one bullet left.

KEATING
They'll show up.

AMBROSE
Yes, but will they show up before I go mad once again?

KEATING
Again?

AMBROSE
Sorry. Didn't I – tell you?

Beat.

KEATING
No.

AMBROSE
No? Really? Oh. I spent two years in a – a hospital, I guess you'd call it. For people who are, uh – you know. Temporarily –

KEATING
You didn't mention this before.

AMBROSE
No; I exaggerate. Nineteen months in all.

KEATING
You're insane?

AMBROSE
Was. Not really insane. Just lost my mind there for a bit. It was that last land survey.

Seeing it once again before him.

Saskatchewan. Bit of topographical hell, really. Like mapping a fucking ocean.

KEATING
So what are you doing out?

AMBROSE
Well. I'm better now. I think.

Beat. WING enters. A thirty-year-old Chinese man, who scuttles from place to place, almost always carrying something. This time, a pail of water.

KEATING
Where have you been, Wong?

AMBROSE
Wing.

KEATING

I've been waiting for my bath. And don't give me that shifty look. He's shifty. Don't be shifty with me. Bath!

AMBROSE

He doesn't understand you. You're going to have to act it out.

KEATING

Act?

AMBROSE

Gesticulate.

KEATING

Oh, for God's sake. Look, you. Bath! Bath! Get it?

He mimes bathing.

AMBROSE

That doesn't look like a bath.

KEATING

Yes it does.

AMBROSE

It looks like a man with epilepsy.

KEATING goes to the large round metal tub, pretends to pour.

KEATING

See? See? Bath. Baaaaaathhhhhhh. He's pretending he doesn't understand. How can you not know what I'm talking about? Put the water in there. It's so basic. You see? He knows what I'm saying. Look. He enjoys this. Let go of that water! He wants me to get into the tub; that's what he wants. Make a tit of myself. I'm not getting in the tub. I'm not. Oh, for God's sake.

He gets into the tub and sits.

There. Happy? Bath!

WING

Ah!

KEATING

See? What did I tell you?

AMBROSE

You do look like a tit, actually.

WING runs off, taking the water with him.

KEATING

Where are you going with that water? What's he doing?

AMBROSE

I didn't think you were that clear, to be honest.

KEATING

It's a game he plays.

AMBROSE

You give him too much credit. I don't think he's that bright.

KEATING

Were you barking mad? Did they lock you in a room?

AMBROSE

Must we discuss this?

KEATING

I want to know.

AMBROSE

Of course they didn't lock me in a room. It was all perfectly civil. I was suffering a kind of nervous exhaustion; that's all. Acting rather strangely, you know: sitting in a tree and not coming down; that sort of thing. And they thought, for the sake of appearances, I ought to go away for a while. My father, as you know, is minister of our congregation. And the tree was beside the church, et cetera.

KEATING
Really?

AMBROSE
You'd be amazed what a year and a half of weaving mats can do.

KEATING
I think you should have told the Major.

AMBROSE
It's irrelevant. Let's just drop it.

KEATING
I'm keeping the gun, if you don't mind.

AMBROSE
Why?

KEATING
In case you go off the rails again.

AMBROSE
You think if I were going to kill you I wouldn't have done it by now?

KEATING
Maybe you're waiting for the right moment.

AMBROSE
So far, I can't think of a wrong moment.

WING enters with two pails this time, emptying them into the metal tub in the middle of the tent. KEATING, meanwhile, strips to his long underwear.

KEATING

There you are. And keep the water coming; not like last time. (*to AMBROSE*) I don't like him. (*to WING*) Yes, yes. Water. Good man.

AMBROSE

Why not?

KEATING

He seems so ill-suited to service. I don't think they get it, frankly – these Orientals. Our superiority is completely lost on them. They know we're in charge, but they don't appreciate why. (*to WING*) And hurry back!

WING runs off.

I wonder if I could ask you a bit of personal favour, Ambrose.

AMBROSE

Don't look at me like that; I'm not lending you my lint brush to clean your teeth again.

KEATING

Listen. I wonder if you could have a quick look at my ass.

AMBROSE

Why?

KEATING

I think I've got a crawly or two down there.

AMBROSE

Really, Keating.

KEATING

Just a quick gander.

Opens the back flap of his underwear.

Please. For heaven's sake. As a gentleman.

AMBROSE
    I can hardly see as it is. Look what's happened to my
    spectacles.

KEATING
    Use the tweezers if you must.

AMBROSE
    I warned you this would happen.

KEATING
    No you didn't. Did you?

AMBROSE
    Whores.

KEATING
    What about them.

AMBROSE
    Let's have a look, then; hurry up. I don't like
    backsides. They remind me too much of – something.
    Home, I think.

      KEATING bends over and AMBROSE takes a sidelong look.

KEATING
    See anything?

AMBROSE
    It's rather dim.

KEATING
    Try the candle.

AMBROSE
    I'm a bit worried about gas.

KEATING
    It's not a Welsh coalmine, for God's sake.

AMBROSE goes in close with a lighted match and pair of tweezers. WING enters with more water, pausing briefly to notice what's going on, then proceeding to pour more water.

KEATING

Any sightings?

AMBROSE

Hardly the sort of wildlife one expects to encounter in these parts. I'm not sure what this is.

KEATING

Is it moving?

AMBROSE

I can't tell.

KEATING

Squish it. OW!

AMBROSE

Sorry. I don't know what that was.

KEATING

The water can't possibly be hot.

AMBROSE

What?

KEATING

I'm talking to him. Don't give me that look. What's he gawking at? The water is not hot. The water is not hot. Hopeless.

AMBROSE

Honestly, I don't see anything.

KEATING

Are you sure?

AMBROSE
I am not getting any closer, Keating. I have reached the boundaries of personal etiquette.

KEATING
I've heard that paraffin is effective.

AMBROSE
Perhaps you should learn to get along with nature.

KEATING
In the first place, nature is not for getting along with; any Englishman knows that. And in the second place – what were we talking about?

AMBROSE
Nature.

KEATING
That's right. Nature – to hell with it. You hear these people going on and on about it. On and on.

AMBROSE
What people?

KEATING
I don't know. God, what an itch. Aren't people going on and on about it? Nature. I can hear them going on and on. Look what a lot of trouble it is. These mountains are a good example.

AMBROSE
Of what?

KEATING
Trouble; what do you think? They're in the way.

AMBROSE
Of what?

KEATING

Stop saying "of what." The railroad, for a start.

AMBROSE

Perhaps the railroad should be going north and south.

KEATING

What on earth are you talking about?

AMBROSE

That's where the valleys are. North and south. Not
east and west. Has it occurred to you? Why are we
going east to west? Why are we going over mountains?

KEATING

What a preposterous question, Ambrose.

AMBROSE

Is it?

KEATING

You're just saying this to upset me.

AMBROSE

Upset you? Not at all.

KEATING

And now, at last, I know the source of this willful
contrariness; you're out of your fucking mind. It's a
matter of record. You've admitted it.

AMBROSE

Perhaps the Major's out of his mind. Perhaps the
railroad is out of its mind.

KEATING

I don't think a railroad can be out of its mind,
technically speaking.

AMBROSE

In a way I think it can. In a way, I think it can become
so twisted and doubled back on itself, that it's insane.
If it represents the thinking of madmen, then it's
bonkers isn't it? Have you asked yourself why we're
doing this?

KEATING

Of course not. I don't need to ask myself every little
thing. I *know* why. Besides, if I asked myself every little
thing, then eventually I would be asking myself why I
was asking myself what I was asking myself – if you see
what I mean. Can you imagine where that would lead?

AMBROSE

No.

KEATING

I'm beginning to think, Ambrose, that you're not
much of an empire builder. Who gives a damn where
valleys are? We're already following the course of a
river; isn't that natural enough? The river ends. What
are we supposed to do? Stop? Just *stop*?!

AMBROSE

I don't know what we're supposed to do.

KEATING

North to south? Who's going in that bloody
direction?

AMBROSE

It's what the Indians have always done; for ages, now.

KEATING

Who gives a damn about Indians?

AMBROSE

True. I'm only wondering why it is that they've never,
in a thousand years, bothered to cross even one of
these stupid great things.

KEATING

Just look at them. Running around in blankets.
Pleased with themselves to sit about cross-legged all
day, content.

AMBROSE

So it's discontent, is it? That drives us onward?

KEATING

We're driven is all that matters. Driven to greatness, I
might add.

AMBROSE

At least I know, now, it's not a complete waste of time,
mapping every square inch of it. From one end to the
other, a railroad will shunt hapless passengers back
and forth, one day, across a landscape so vast it defies
reason; leaving a nation scratching its head. People
will at last be confronted with their own pointlessness.
Why? Discontent.

KEATING

So long as they name a mountain after me, I don't
give a damn.

AMBROSE

I think you have to climb a mountain in order to have
it named for you.

KEATING

No, Ambrose. I think you only have to spot it.

AMBROSE

That's stars you're thinking of. I believe if you check
in the Brainless Bastard's Manual of Vainglorious and

Idiotic Pursuits, you'll find specific instructions. Not only do you have to get to the top of a mountain, I think you have to stick a flag in it, Keating. We don't have a flag.

KEATING

I've spotted my mountain already. Actually, two mountains together. Those ones over there that look like a pair of tits.

AMBROSE

I could have guessed. The ones you've been obsessing about for a week.

KEATING

I haven't been obsessing about them. I find them attractive, certainly; even captivating. And in a certain light, at dusk, if you squint, you could almost be forgiven for thinking that you were looking up at the bosom of a female colossus, as she reclined, naked, on the evergreen divan of an Olympian shag house; her nipples white with Apollo's glistening – well, you get the picture.

AMBROSE

Yes.

KEATING

I find it interesting that you're not aroused by the sight of a woman's breasts, Ambrose.

AMBROSE

I find it interesting that you are. After all, they're mountains.

KEATING

Mountains. Exactly.

KEATING goes to look out the tent flap.

Well, he's gone off now, and he won't come back.
The fellow has no sense of timing. Where does he go
to, anyway? There's no bloody place to go; where does
he go?

AMBROSE points to a silhouette on the canvas.

AMBROSE
He's right there.

KEATING
What's he doing?

AMBROSE
I suppose he's waiting for your water to boil.

KEATING
Look at him.

AMBROSE
Poor stupid bastard.

KEATING
Well, I'm not having a bath. By the time that's ready,
this'll be cold. He really should have had four or five
kettles going at once. To hell with it.

AMBROSE
Tell him to stop, then.

KEATING
Why? He's not doing anything else.

He sprawls on his cot.

AMBROSE
I suppose not. I suppose it's better to imagine you're
useful than to know you're not.

KEATING
Sitting there, ruminating. I don't like the way he sits
and ruminates. What on earth could he possibly have
to think about?

AMBROSE
Maybe he thinks about you.

KEATING
What would he think?

AMBROSE
What a large cauliflower your head looks like.

KEATING
He'd better fucking not.
    He thinks.
They are a lovely pair of tits, though.

AMBROSE
Yes. What'll you call them?

KEATING
Keating's Titties, I was thinking.

AMBROSE
Confusing.

KEATING
How?

AMBROSE
They're not really yours. People a hundred years from
now will stop and wonder why you had tits like a
woman's.

KEATING
I see your point.

AMBROSE
How about Keating's Favourite Titties?

KEATING
Bit of a mouthful.

AMBROSE
I'd say.

KEATING
Since we're being philosophical, do you mind if I ask you a question?

AMBROSE
No, I don't think there's a civilization on the moon entirely of naked women.

KEATING
I wasn't going to ask you that.

AMBROSE
Good.

KEATING
Alright, I was going to ask you that; but since you clearly don't want to discuss it, how about this God thing, then. Do you really not believe in God, Ambrose? Seriously? It's so obvious there is one.

AMBROSE
What's your evidence?

KEATING
Evidence? I don't have any evidence. It's just obvious.

AMBROSE
Well, you have to have evidence.

KEATING
Why?

AMBROSE
Like everything else, Keating, the facts have to bear a thing out. You're a man of science. Sort of.

KEATING
But according to your theory, after we die, we just disintegrate into nothing. How is that possible? Besides, it's so childish and boring to want evidence of everything. *Evidence.*

AMBROSE
Couldn't we talk about something else? Or better yet, nothing else.

KEATING
And your father, a minister.

AMBROSE
I can't help that.

KEATING
Have you discussed this with him?

AMBROSE
Well, he's awfully busy with his affairs. Got two going on at the moment.

KEATING
What? With women? No.

AMBROSE
Maybe three. There's the Jamaican housekeeper, the turnip girl, when she's available. Sorry, the third one jumped off a cliff; dressed in a toga.

KEATING
Well, it's clear that the reason you no longer believe in God is that your father let you down, you see.

AMBROSE

I see.

KEATING

Father, God. Get it?

AMBROSE

Is that it? Oh. I thought it might be that if I believed
in God, I'd be forced to believe he was a thoughtless
twit who neglected the suffering of his own children,
and insisted that people sing songs of praise about
him, while pontificating about selflessness. You're
right. He is like my father.

KEATING

Let me tell you a story.

AMBROSE

Oh, look. I've fallen asleep.

KEATING

No you haven't. You're talking.

AMBROSE

I'm talking in my sleep.

KEATING

If you don't believe in God, then you can't possibly
believe in destiny. Just think about it, Ambrose. What
would be the point of anything? We wouldn't be
building railroads across continents. We'd be
miserable wretches sitting in grimy cafés in bloody
Paris, dreaming of Utopia. *This* is Utopia. Not the
world as it should be; the world as it will be.

AMBROSE snores, but KEATING continues, unperturbed.

Go ahead and snort all you like. I hate the city. I
despise the thinking but not doing of things. It may
come as a surprise to you, but I'm not much of an

intellectual, when it comes right down to it. Still, I have my philosophy, and it's this: A man – a man must – he must strive – a man must strive to – to – I don't really have a philosophy. In fact, that's my philosophy, as it turns out. No philosophy at all. Who needs a stupid philosophy when you've got an axe? By the time they've thought of a reason for it, we'll already have chopped our way from one end of this frozen shit hole to the other. What a lovely idea for a song.

Noticing AMBROSE asleep, he sneaks over and has a look at his journal.

"I feel the madness oozing in me, now, like hot wax." How on earth do you know what hot wax feels like oozing in you? "But this time, I let it flow; I let it flow." Not on my watch.

Finding the gun, he removes the single bullet, and pockets it. WING enters with water.

What do you want? I'm not having a bath, now. Not having one. Not – having – a bath! Understand?

WING
Ah.

WING pours the water into the bath. Blackout.

Scene Two

Many days later; October actually. KEATING is stripping for his bath, as WING waits, with towel, taking his underwear, going out for more water, etc. AMBROSE writes in his journal.

KEATING
Have you given any thought to why the guide fucked off last week?

AMBROSE
No.

KEATING
I have. I've been giving it considerable thought. He was French; did you know that?

AMBROSE
No.

KEATING
He was French. They hate the English. Why? No reason. Jealousy, I expect. Stupidity. Frenchness. But here's my theory – you didn't get that he was French?

AMBROSE
Yes, I knew he was French.

KEATING
What gave you your first clue?

AMBROSE
He spoke it.

KEATING
You know what tipped me off? His poncey hair. The
French all have greasy, poncey hair. Or is that the
Italians? Look at how irritated and full of air he gets,
Wing. I say the slightest thing and he blows himself up
like a balloon. I only do it to watch your face go all
red. My theory is that the bastard was working for the
fur trade. You know what those boys are like. The last
thing they want is a railroad through here. They'll be
out of business. Speculators, trappers, all of them,
pushed aside by the great surge, the great wash of
humanity, flooding into these valleys. This'll be an
English country; not a fucking French one. Bastards.
You hear that, Wing? An English country. Get my
guitar. Don't just stand there! I feel the lyric muse. My
guitar, you stupid twat! I taught him the word.

AMBROSE
"Twat"?

KEATING
He knows what I'm saying. Watch this. Gui – tar!

AMBROSE
Maybe he just doesn't care.

WING
Ah.

KEATING
You see.

WING exits.

Oh, for fuck's sake.

43

A beat. AMBROSE writes; KEATING watches.

Still feeling suicidal?

AMBROSE
Whatever gave you the idea I was suicidal?

KEATING
I don't know.

AMBROSE
I haven't mentioned anything about it.

KEATING
Perhaps I sensed you were.

AMBROSE
Well, I'm not.

KEATING
Oh.

AMBROSE
Have you been looking at my journal?

KEATING
Why would I?

AMBROSE
Because it's so like you.

KEATING
That scribbling, blotchy, unreadable mess? You think
I don't have some sense of propriety? I'm the model
of it. I was surprised to discover what you think of
me, though.

AMBROSE
You *know* what I think of you. It couldn't be clearer
if I hired a company of Italian pantomimers to act it
out.

KEATING

    You go about pretending you loathe the sight of me,
    and yet you harbour these secret – how should I put
    it? – emotions.

AMBROSE

    Emotions? I've only got one.

KEATING

    Say what you like, but I've read your heart-felt
    confession. "I would desperately love Keating, but
    cannot be bothered to act upon it."

AMBROSE

    Where did you read that?

KEATING

    October 5th. It's a little smudged, but it made me
    blush all the same.

      AMBROSE flips to the date.

AMBROSE

    October 5th. That's, "I would desperately love to
    murder Keating, but cannot be bothered to act upon
    it." You're right. It is heart-felt.

KEATING

    Murder?

AMBROSE

    Figure of speech. As it goes on to say, "I couldn't be
    bothered."

KEATING

    Well, I won't ask you what a "thwill quag moron" is,
    then. Obviously not what I thought.

AMBROSE

    Now your feelings are hurt.

KEATING

They're not.

AMBROSE

They are.

KEATING

A little.

AMBROSE

If I were a person who had any kindness in him at all,
I would apologize at this point; I'd probably say
something like "sorry."

KEATING

And I would probably say "I accept"; or something to
that effect.

AMBROSE

Good. Let's just leave it at that; a theoretical apology
and acceptance. It would help, in the future, though,
if you kept your nose out of my BLOODY JOURNAL!

KEATING

I don't know what else I'm supposed to read. A
German Bible? The longer they take to get here, the
worse it gets. I'm quite pleased, I have to say, with
how this thread works on the teeth, though. You
could make money off this. Sell it in shops.

AMBROSE

It's thread. They already sell it in shops. Where did
you get that, by the way? That's not mine, is it?

KEATING

My buttons, where else?

AMBROSE

And how are you keeping your buttons on?

KEATING

I'm not.

AMBROSE

That's not really thinking ahead, is it?

KEATING

Who's thinking ahead? All I can think about at the
moment are these burns on my bottom.

AMBROSE

I told you not to use paraffin.

KEATING

It wasn't so much the paraffin, it was the match. And
all that's happened is, they've run round to the front,
now. You have no idea what my balls feel like,
Ambrose. Never mind, I'll tell you. Like I've been
wearing pants made of nettles. I've scratched so much
they look like a pair of Christmas tree ornaments.
The left one, especially –

AMBROSE

Surely to God, man, there's a subject of conversation
we could engage in, for *once*, that doesn't involve your
testicles!

KEATING

Do we have any kerosene?

AMBROSE

I wasn't feeling suicidal.

KEATING

No?

AMBROSE

I was referring to men in general, not one in
particular. I was asking myself what the true meaning
of one's life is. The altitude brought it on.

KEATING

Meaning of one's life?

AMBROSE

I've decided, I don't want to wait until the Major gets
here to have a discussion about it, I'm heading back.

KEATING

Back?

AMBROSE

To the coast. I've experienced enough futility out
here to last me a lifetime. There must be something
more a man can accomplish than this. It isn't the
waiting, I realize. It's the *doing*, when the waiting is
over. We'll find a pass through the range, they'll build
a railroad after us, and then what? History will move
forward, dragging us along with it. But we'll still have
our – lives to live.

KEATING

You really don't like that fiancée of yours, do you?

AMBROSE

I'd rather marry a herd of mountain goats.

KEATING

You're joking about that.

AMBROSE

I'm not going back home. I've decided that, too. I'll
set out to sea. I won't come back to land, ever again. I
hate land; every measured-out little inch of it. I came
out here to be free. To feel what it feels like to be
unfettered. There's no such thing.

KEATING

I can't allow you to go before the Major gets here.

AMBROSE
    Try and stop me.

    AMBROSE marches over and grabs the rifle.

KEATING
    What are you doing?

AMBROSE
    I'll hang on to this, for now.

KEATING
    You'll never find your way back. You're frightened of
    squirrels, for God's sake.

AMBROSE
    Squirrels have rabies!

KEATING
    I should know, I was the one that got bitten.

AMBROSE
    You won't stand in my way.

KEATING
    There's only one bullet in that thing.

AMBROSE
    Don't make me use it before I leave.

KEATING
    Go ahead.

AMBROSE
    You're awfully brave.

    WING enters.

KEATING
    Look, Wing. He's threatening to shoot me.

AMBROSE
No I'm not.

KEATING
I've a witness.

AMBROSE
Don't be stupid. I'm not going to shoot you.

KEATING
I think you should shoot me.

AMBROSE
I don't want to.

KEATING
I want you to.

AMBROSE
I don't want to.

KEATING
Then shoot *him*.

AMBROSE
Why?

KEATING
Because you're insane, Ambrose. You said so yourself.

WING
Ohhhh.

KEATING
Shut up, you.

AMBROSE
No one's shooting anybody. I'm just hanging on to
this so you won't prevent me from leaving when I do.
And I never, ever said I was insane. I said I spent
nineteen months in an asylum.

KEATING gets out of the tub, toweling himself, getting dressed.

KEATING

We're contracted to be here. You can't run out like this.

AMBROSE

Oh, I will. I'll run out just like this. In fact, I'm going now. What are we doing, Keating? Try asking yourself that. Fifty-one degrees north, one hundred and eighteen degrees west; what does it bloody matter? Do you really imagine they're going to name a mountain after you, let alone two? You'll be lucky if they honour you with so much as a pile of wet leaves. Keating's Pile of Soggy Wet Leaves, turn left, one mile. Even if there were any glory in this, it won't belong to you. They'll name it all after the Royal fucking Family as usual. *Keating?* You must be joking. You'll be dropped off the roster like the bastard at a family reunion. The only way you'll make history is if you take this gun and shoot the Major in the head, the minute he rounds the mountain. Even then, they'll call it Shot in the Head Pass or something. But at least you'll have made your mark.

KEATING

What an appalling lack of vision. Is it any wonder the Scots are all stuck up there in – ?

An effort.

AMBROSE

Scotland.

KEATING

This isn't about me. This is – well, alright, it's about me. But it's about so much more. It's about fearlessness; it's about forging ahead, you idiot; it's

about – I have no idea what it's about, but *they* do;
dammit.

AMBROSE

Who?

KEATING

That lot. The ones who – come up with these
things. Who cares what it means? Do you really
need it all to make sense? Does – does the bloody
Roman bloody Panthenon make sense?

AMBROSE

Parthenon. It's in Athens.

KEATING

What is?

AMBROSE

The Parthenon is in Athens.

KEATING

There you go again. I don't care if it's under your hat;
it's still the Panthenon.

AMBROSE

Parthenon.

KEATING

What's the point of it? It's there; that's all.

AMBROSE

It was the seat of the first democracy.

KEATING

Besides all that. It's just a pile of old – have you seen
it? Breathtaking. But what's the point? Who gives a
damn? It's there! Plonk down in the middle of – you
know –

AMBROSE
Mm.

KEATING
Athens?

AMBROSE
I've actually lost track of what we were talking about.

KEATING
So have I.

AMBROSE
Oh, that's right. I was going.

KEATING
You're staying. We're a team. Otherwise, it's just him.

AMBROSE
What's wrong with him?

KEATING
We don't get along.

AMBROSE
You don't get along with me, either.

KEATING
But you're not Chinese.

AMBROSE
That's another thing. What have you got against the Chinese?

KEATING
Nothing; obviously. But I like an intellectual challenge. You challenge me, intellectually. Look at him.

They consider WING, as he stands, waiting.

AMBROSE
>Well, I can't do anything about him. Besides, he's
>your man.

KEATING
>No, he isn't. He's your man.

AMBROSE
>No he isn't.

KEATING
>Well, whose man is he?

>>*Beat.*

>Look here! Whose man are you?

WING
>Ah!

>>*He rushes off.*

AMBROSE
>You're joking.

KEATING
>Well, he's somebody's.

AMBROSE
>Is he?

KEATING
>Oh, balls.

>>*Another beat as they think it through.*

AMBROSE
>Anyway, he can keep you company while you wait for
>that megalomaniacal gasbag of a Major to finally
>present himself.

KEATING
Is that what you think of the great man?

AMBROSE
Yes.

KEATING attacks his genitals.

KEATING
Damn these crawly creatures.

AMBROSE starts packing some things into a bag.

AMBROSE
Worse than that, he's an American. Which means that in his own sweet sentimental way, he'll pull the whole thing off with great aplomb and make everybody feel brilliantly fantastic. Besides, I can't abide the way he wears his hat. Jaunty, like a woman.

KEATING
It suits him.

AMBROSE
Here. I'm leaving you my Baxter lithograph of Botticelli's Venus.

KEATING
Say what you like, I admire him.

AMBROSE
Of course you do. Why wouldn't you? He's an inspiration to us all. Like a rousing great anthem. Everybody leaping to their feet, and off we go over the mountain.

KEATING
He's a father figure. That's why you don't like him.

AMBROSE

You're right.

KEATING

You can disagree with me all you want, but a pattern is emerging here.

AMBROSE

I said "You're right."

KEATING

Go ahead and – and – what?

AMBROSE

I agree with you.

KEATING

Only for sake of argument.

AMBROSE

He reminds me of my father, that's right. You've got me all figured out. I'll leave the gun at the bottom of the path, by the river. Don't follow me.

AMBROSE is packed and ready to go.

KEATING

Can I offer you a word of advice?

AMBROSE

No.

KEATING

What if you run into a grizzly?

AMBROSE

Doesn't matter.

KEATING

This is desertion, Ambrose.

AMBROSE
> We're not in the army.

KEATING
> We're soldiers for progress. Rouse yourself, for God's
> sake. Whatever happened to "Once more unto the
> breach" and all that? What day is it today? The
> fourth?

AMBROSE
> Twelfth.

KEATING
> Even better. The twelfth. Remember this day. From
> this day forward, it'll be the day that all men speak of.
> The twelfth. The day we few, we valiant few, we men
> of England (and some of Scotland – and one of
> China, if we're including him) –

AMBROSE
> If they're not here in a week, head back.

KEATING
> I can't do that. It's an obligation.

AMBROSE
> Leave the equipment; leave our work. The route
> back to the coast is marked. If you wait for another
> snowfall, you won't get out.

KEATING
> I don't want to get out.

AMBROSE
> What?

KEATING
> I want to go forward. Ever forward.

AMBROSE

Well, I want to go back.

KEATING

Forward.

AMBROSE

Back.

KEATING

Do you suppose this is what they mean by "the great divide"?

AMBROSE

Adieu.

KEATING

We owe it to the generations that follow, Ambrose.

AMBROSE

How can you be so deluded?

KEATING

Deluded? You call it a delusion to think of yourself as one of the great men of history? Imagine some stupid soldier in Alexander's conquering army, droning on about the "pointlessness" of ruling the world. This is greater than both of us, Ambrose. This is a *topographical survey*!

AMBROSE

I only mean this to be kind, Keating. When I've gone, take the gun and shoot yourself. It'll be over quick and you won't have to spend the rest of your life being, well, you. As for me, I'm going. Nothing will stop me. Nothing.

KEATING

What'll I tell the Major?

AMBROSE

On the off chance that he's even listening, tell him
it's all a myth; this whole toe-freezing enterprise. But
then he knows that. The man's an Olympian. Forging
together a nation with his bare hands. But he won't
manage it. Do you know what a nation is, Keating? It's
a people. Not a railroad. Not this longitude or this
latitude. We drew these lines! Is this real? Or a bunch
of profiteers, in beaver hats? Ask him how we can
presume to map out a future, without taking into
account the past. They want to build a fantasyland
here, Keating. Push aside a real people to put in an
imaginary one. Tell him they won't do it. Because in
order to build a great lie of a country, you need a
population that lies to itself. And that won't happen.
Oh. And when you're finished with all that, ask him if
he wouldn't mind fucking off back to America, with
all the rest of the great nation builders; and leave this
wasteland as it is.

KEATING

I could just say hello.

AMBROSE

Say what you like.

AMBROSE leaves.

*KEATING stands in the middle of the tent, pondering his
future. WING enters with water bucket. Wonders what's
happened.*

KEATING

Well don't just stand there.

*Outside, a low rumble, which builds and builds into a
roaring thunder. An enormous slide. KEATING and WING
take cover. The slide over, they emerge from hiding.*

WING

    Yau mo gau cho.

KEATING

    I couldn't have said it better myself.

    AMBROSE appears, with great effort dragging himself into the tent, covered in dirt and dust. He stops and looks at KEATING.

KEATING

    No way back, now.

AMBROSE

    No way forward, either.

    Blackout. Interval.

Scene Three

*AMBROSE is trussed up in some sort of makeshift leg cast,
writing in his journal; occasionally he winces with pain.
KEATING sits on his cot, strumming the guitar.*

KEATING

I was itchin', I was itchin', I was itchin' for my darling. I
got trapped in the mountains, and I wrote myself this
song. Oh, an av'lanche came down whilst my friend
and I were quar'ling. (*waiting for AMBROSE to comment*)

AMBROSE

I didn't say anything.

KEATING

Poetic licence it's called.

AMBROSE

I wonder why it's not called "crap licence"?

KEATING

I'm trying to keep my mind off my balls.

AMBROSE

I think we all feel that way.

KEATING

The burning almost goes away if I sing.

AMBROSE

That was the last of the kerosene, as well.

KEATING
    I find I have to think of something extraordinary.
    Guess what I'm thinking about.

AMBROSE
    A woman with incredibly large tits?

KEATING
    My God. That's uncanny.

AMBROSE
    Too bad about your mountain.

KEATING
    You wouldn't think the landscape could be so altered
    by one landslide. Looks more like a gigantic bum
    sticking up in the air, now. I'm naming it after my
    own true love.

AMBROSE
    The Girl Who Gave Me Crabs Mountain?

KEATING
    Melinda's Backside.

AMBROSE
    What time is it?

KEATING
    What difference does it make?

AMBROSE
    I've got a schedule. I'm allowing myself to scream
    with pain every hour on the hour.

KEATING
    It's three.

        AMBROSE lets out a great shout.

AMBROSE
There. Did you climb up to the lookout, yet?

KEATING
The what?

AMBROSE
Lookout.

KEATING
I sent Wing.

AMBROSE
Wing?

KEATING
He'll report back.

AMBROSE
In Chinese?

KEATING thinks about that.

What about the fire? Did you get some smoke going?

KEATING
I sent out two signals today already. I think they were
signals. How do you spell "predicament"?

AMBROSE
Did you use the mirror?

KEATING
It's not very sunny out.

AMBROSE
Sorry, but you tend to sit there, doing nothing most
of the time. I think you should be taking *this* a little
more seriously than your singed scrotum. If they're in
the vicinity –

KEATING
They'll find us if they're in the vicinity.

AMBROSE
How? We're completely surrounded by fallen rock.

KEATING
I've got a plan.

AMBROSE
No you don't.

KEATING
Would you like to hear it?

AMBROSE
No. Yes. No.

KEATING
The plan is this. The plan as I see it. Are you listening? What we'll do is – it's simple. What we'll do – it's really quite straightforward, so don't get all – we're going to – to formulate a – what's it called – formulate – a sort of –

AMBROSE
Plan?

KEATING
No. A *strategy*.

    Beat.

AMBROSE
I see. The plan is to make a strategy.

KEATING
I haven't finished.

AMBROSE
Brilliant.

KEATING

> Details need to be ironed out. Don't give me that look.

AMBROSE

> Here. I've got a plan. We die of starvation, and then we lie about for a bit, and then we rot. Why don't you do something constructive and go hit yourself over the head repeatedly with a piece of shale.

KEATING

> I just had a profound thought. What if they *don't* find us.

AMBROSE

> It's what I just said. That's not even a thought, let alone a profound one.

> *WING enters, with a dead gopher.*

KEATING

> There you are.

> *Smiling, WING presents the rodent.*

> What's this?

AMBROSE

> His report, obviously.

KEATING

> I didn't want a fucking dead rodent! I wanted you on lookout. Your language skills seriously need some work! Get that away from me.

AMBROSE

> I think it's quite thoughtful. Thank you, Wing. Very nice.

> *WING starts to cry.*

> Look. Now you've upset the poor stupid bastard.

KEATING
    What are we supposed to do? Eat this?!

AMBROSE
    We've not much else, to be honest. A half a pot of
    quince jam and three tins of Mrs. Wilton's Minced
    Kidney Jelly.

KEATING
    (*sheepishly*) Two. (*turning on WING*) Stop blubbering,
    you! It's not the English way.

AMBROSE
    At least he's trying. There's a good boy. Fry that up,
    now, and we'll have some tea.

KEATING
    I'm not eating a rat for tea. I'm going out to catch a
    goat.

WING
    Ngoh m ming baak.

AMBROSE
    You haven't got the slightest idea how to catch a goat.
    Anyway, they're sheep.

KEATING
    You take it by its back legs, if you must know, and
    swing it round and round, into the side of a cliff.
    What could be simpler?

AMBROSE
    Can I've your portion of this, then?

KEATING
    By the way, I've decided to take exception to what you
    said a few days ago.

AMBROSE

Really? About what?

KEATING

You *seemed* to be implying that our work here is
worthless.

AMBROSE

I don't think I was implying that. I think I was stating
it directly.

KEATING

Well, perhaps we should debate this further, Ambrose.
Since we have the time.

AMBROSE

Don't you have a goat to catch?

KEATING

First of all, what we're doing is not worthless in that
we're getting paid for it; so there goes your argument
right there. Second of all, consider your present
situation and ponder the following. You very well may
not get out of here. Why? Well, because, because even
when the Major shows up as surely he will, how do you
propose we're going to get you back? Our horses, as
you know, have disappeared under a large fucking
heap of rocks. The Major's unlikely to have extra ones
– you know how he is about that; so what do you
imagine the procedure is for transporting a man with
a broken leg through the mountains? Let me give you
a hint. There isn't one. As for Wing and I, well, we'll
be expected to hop it back on foot; but what about
you? What'll you hop it back on? Your head? But wait.
I haven't begun to make my argument. It's very likely,
if things turn out the way I expect they will, that you

will not be leaving here, Ambrose, at all; whether the Major arrives or not. History, in this case, is not on your side. Were it, say, twenty years from now, and there were, say, a *railroad* running through this wasteland as you like to call it, then no problem. Pop you on board and off you go, back home. But there is no railroad, sorry. Why? It's not built yet. Point taken? You talk about worthless ventures. I think your life is a bit of a worthless venture at this point. Sorry. I just wanted to apprise you of the tragicomedy of the situation here. You appear to have hoisted yourself on your own – thingamajig.

AMBROSE
You wouldn't leave me.

KEATING
I wouldn't leave you; don't be absurd. But it won't be up to me. We'll vote as a group, of course. You know what the Major's like.

AMBROSE
Democratic twat.

KEATING
Public opinion will not be on your side. Sorry. However, a note of consolation here.

AMBROSE
What's that?

KEATING
We haven't used that bullet, yet.

A wolf howls. Fade to black.

Scene Four

*AMBROSE sleeps in his cot. WING watches him. He hears
KEATING coming, and slips out of the tent. In a moment,
KEATING, a wild look in his eyes, enters covered in snow.
He has the gun.*

KEATING
    Wake up!

AMBROSE
    Huh?

KEATING
    I said "Wake up."

AMBROSE
    What in God's name?

KEATING
    I want to report my findings.

    AMBROSE pulls himself up, waking.

AMBROSE
    Yes?

KEATING
    Nothing.

AMBROSE
    Sorry?

KEATING

Not a thing. Bugger all.

AMBROSE

Ah.

KEATING

Thought you should know.

AMBROSE

Thank you. So; not much to report.

KEATING

I didn't say there was not much to report. I said "nothing." Got me? "Not *much*" would suggest the tiniest of somethings. I've been standing up on the lookout, now, for three hours or maybe three days, I don't know which. I found a crow. Which I considered attaching a note to; but it was dead. I saw one of those – what-do-you-call-its with the things – I saw some deer droppings. So – we've got lunch taken care of. And I saw lots and lots and lots and lots of snow. Oh, and at one point, at very close range, I thought I spotted a Big Horn sheep, but it just turned out to be a man in a coolie hat, squatting for a wizz. I decided not to shoot, in the end.

AMBROSE

You woke me up to report nothing.

KEATING

That's right. No. As a matter of fact, I woke you up because I felt like it. Because I don't want you sleeping anymore. No, that's not it. I woke you up because I've had an idea. What is it? Oh, yeah. You might think it's a bit grand, this – knowing you – but I've had the idea of building a kind of hot air balloon thing.

AMBROSE

Well, except for the hot air part and the balloon part,
I think you're onto something.

KEATING

You have to exercise some imagination in situations
like these. Look at you, lying about like a sultan,
criticizing my every idea. Alright. So we don't have a
balloon. What about this tent?

AMBROSE

Where are your pants?

KEATING

They fell off.

AMBROSE

Why?

KEATING

Why else; I used all the thread on my teeth.

AMBROSE

Sorry; didn't mean to interrupt. Do go on. You were
making a balloon out of the tent.

KEATING

Was I? That's a good idea.

Beat.

AMBROSE

When was the last time you ate?

KEATING

I can't remember.

AMBROSE

You seem a bit – light-headed today. Why don't you
eat? Oh, that's right – there isn't anything. You don't
look very good, you know.

KEATING

Well, neither do you.

AMBROSE

I think I have gangrene.

KEATING

Really? That doesn't sound very nice.

AMBROSE

It isn't.

KEATING

So what do you want me to do about it?

AMBROSE

I'm not sure, but I think you might have to cut off
my leg.

KEATING

Right.

> *KEATING faints.*

AMBROSE

Oh, for God's sake. It's not your bloody leg. Get up.
He's really going off the deep end. I'd better have
that gun, quick. Wing! Wing!

> *WING runs in.*

Hurry up. Get me his gun!

WING

O?

AMBROSE

His gun!

> *WING removes KEATING's fur hat.*

Gun. Bang, bang. See? There. Get it.

WING understands, now, about the gun, but unsure what to do. Retrieving it from KEATING, he points it at him.

No, no. Just give it to me. Me!

Unsure, WING now points the gun at AMBROSE.

Jesus. No. Don't point it. Give it. Here, stupid.

KEATING, suddenly waking, wildly wrestles the gun away from WING. Finally, KEATING has the gun, and WING is down.

KEATING
My God, he was about to kill you. Do you realize?

AMBROSE
I asked him to get the gun.

KEATING
    Why?

AMBROSE
In the interests of safety. You nearly fired it when you fainted; blew your own head off.

KEATING
Look at him. He hates me.

WING
Da boon jao, gwei lo.

KEATING
I understood that.

AMBROSE
I don't think he hates you. It's a cultural thing. Put the gun down.

KEATING
(*to WING*) You want to be court-martialled?

AMBROSE
Leave him.

KEATING
Right, then. Where were we?

AMBROSE
My leg.

KEATING
Your leg.

Beat.

What about it?

AMBROSE
Gangrene.

KEATING
Right. What do we do?

AMBROSE
I'm not sure.

Beat.

Cut it off?

Beat.

Quickly?

KEATING
Alright. Let's get busy. No point sitting around talking
about it. Who wants to talk about cutting off a leg?
Wing! Yu chau mau chau chau chau!

WING
E?

AMBROSE
What on earth are you saying?

KEATING
  Don't worry. He understands.

AMBROSE
  Maybe you should sit down for a minute and collect
  your thoughts.

KEATING
  Not at all. Let's get on with it.

AMBROSE
  It needs to be disinfected.

KEATING
  Don't be ridiculous. I've done this before.

AMBROSE
  Is that right?

KEATING
  A thousand times. All you do is take a knife, like this
  one, here –

WING
  Mud liu ah!?

AMBROSE
  Wait. I don't think we should do this.

KEATING
  Why not?

AMBROSE
  Because, because I'm not quite ready. I need some
  time to collect myself. Say – a month.

KEATING
  They'll be here before that.

AMBROSE
  Who?

KEATING

Who do you think?

AMBROSE

Have you considered – the other possibility?

KEATING

What's that?

AMBROSE

Clearly there's been some terrible mistake in
planning. It's the end of November, Keating. We were
meeting up in the first week of September.

KEATING

Oh, all these dates. September, November, Remember
– no. What comes after November?

AMBROSE

December.

KEATING

Are you sure?

AMBROSE

We need to look at the facts.

KEATING

That is so like you, Ambrose. To pin us down with
your annoying encumbrances. Months, days. What do
they mean? Do you know that in a few years' time,
we'll be able to cross this whole continent in four
days? What will a month mean, then? What will
anything mean? Distance, time, will all evaporate in a
– in a – in something. You need to dispense with
these little teensy weensy ideas once and for all. What
will it take for you to see the larger picture?

AMBROSE

A rabid squirrel bite?

KEATING

    What does that mean?

AMBROSE

    Nothing.

KEATING

    You think there's something wrong with me.

AMBROSE

    Not at all.

KEATING

    Go on. You can be honest. Do you think there's
    something wrong with me? Aside from some paralysis
    in my toes and a mild fever?

AMBROSE

    No.

KEATING

    You're just saying that so I won't shoot you.

AMBROSE

    No. Really. Nothing wrong with you.

    Pause.

KEATING

    Good. Because for a moment, I thought there might
    be.

AMBROSE

    Really.

KEATING

    I've been having the strangest dreams. You might
    even say they're not dreams. Because I tend to have
    them while I'm awake, see. Only kidding; wanted to
    see your reaction. No – but the truth is, I heard a
    voice yesterday. And the voice said, "What's going on

here? What's happening?" Only it was with an
American accent, which I can't do very well but there
you are; so I thought, Christ, it's the Major, because it
sounded so very much like him. But when I turned
around – did I tell you this? You're looking at me like
"He told me this, the stupid bastard." No? Well, when
I turned around, what do you think it was? A rock.
Look at you. All concerned that I'm losing my mind.
That's my point, see. I didn't answer it. It was a rock.

Blackout.

Scene Five

AMBROSE writes in his journal. KEATING strums his guitar, singing. He is shaking a little with a fever.

KEATING

Oh, Melinda, oh my deary, is the song that I sing. I've a fever and I'm weary, and my lips are all ting – g'ling, g'ling.

A look to AMBROSE, who smiles his approval.

Just let me know when you want that leg off.

AMBROSE

You'll be the first.

KEATING

What are you writing? It's not about me, is it?

AMBROSE

It's sort of a – what would you call it?

KEATING

Poem?

AMBROSE

Eulogy.

KEATING

Come now. There's no need for that. You know, as well as I do, that things always turn out for the best. Look what happened to Napoleon. I don't mean

Napoleon; who do I mean? No; I mean Napoleon.
Just when all was lost at Waterloo, look what
happened.

AMBROSE
He was defeated?

KEATING
But then he ended up on that little island in the
Mediterranean. All warm and lovely. Why did I bring
that up? I can't remember.

AMBROSE
Neither can I.

KEATING
Thoughts, eh? The mind. Why do I keep forgetting
things?

  Beat.

What things?

  WING enters with soup.

WING
Sic fan may?

KEATING
Get away from me. I don't want that.

AMBROSE
It's quite good. Have you tried it?

KEATING
What is it? He's trying to poison us, and take over.

AMBROSE
Take over what?

KEATING
That's what I've been wondering.

AMBROSE
He manages to catch birds, somehow. They're not
bad.

KEATING
Jau, jua, jua, jua!

WING leaves it and runs off in confusion.

AMBROSE
That's not Chinese.

KEATING
Yes it is.

AMBROSE
Where did you learn it?

KEATING
It's quite simple.

AMBROSE goes back to his eulogy.

AMBROSE
I wonder if those bastards at home will shed a single
tear for me. I wasn't well-liked, as you can imagine.
Tolerated; but not liked. Ignored. Worse, in a way,
than being hated. People smiled, but you knew what
they were thinking. "Topographer." I'm glad I left
there when I did. I don't want them looking at my
dead body. Remarking. "He looks himself." Dreary lot.

KEATING
(*sings*) Oh, Melinda, Melinda – mmm, mm.

He hums under AMBROSE's speech.

AMBROSE
Not a one of them has ever left that stupid town. I'm
the only one. Not for the sake of curiosity, though.
Just to get away from the place. Get out and –

measure. No equivocation. No doubt. No God. Just the rise and gentle fall of the earth, drawn out on paper, with perfect and painstaking exactitude – the infallible tools of science. Maybe they were right, in the end, to stay. What is there in this venture that isn't an illusion? We know exactly and precisely where we are, and it is nowhere at all.

KEATING stops abruptly.

KEATING
Look. I can't move my arms.

Blackout.

Scene Six

KEATING lies in his cot, shaking with a fever. AMBROSE lies in the other cot with a knife, WING standing beside him.

AMBROSE
　　Just cut along here.

WING
　　E?

AMBROSE
　　Leg. Look. See? Cut!

WING
　　Gau hmm dap bah!

AMBROSE
　　This is my only chance, Wing. You've got to do this.

WING
　　Mm.

KEATING
　　(*suddenly, bolting upright*) I've got it. I've got it. I know where the Major is. How could we have been so stupid? He's waiting for us on the moon. My God, we've miscalculated by a long shot.

AMBROSE

> (*to KEATING*) Yes, by a long shot. (*to WING*) Here;
> couple of screams, bit of blood, some hacking and
> sawing, it'll be over.

KEATING

> Hello, mother. What are you doing here?

AMBROSE

> (*to WING*) It's just the rabies. Carry on.

WING

> E?

KEATING

> This is my dear friend, Ambrose. Where are you,
> Ambrose? Ambrose?

AMBROSE

> I'm right here.

KEATING

> What's happening?

AMBROSE

> Well – it's good news and it's bad news.

KEATING

> What's the good news?

AMBROSE

> You haven't got long to live.

KEATING

> In that case, I've got to get up there.

> *Rolling out of bed, he falls.*

> What's happened to my legs?

AMBROSE

> Paralysis, I expect.

KEATING
 Nonsense; I can't feel a thing. What we'll do is this.
 I've got the whole thing worked out. First, we'll need
 to go up the mountain, of course.

AMBROSE
 What? Up Melinda's Bum?

KEATING
 Right up. We'll wait there until the moon is very low
 on the horizon. We'll use rope. Chuck it across. What
 do you think?

AMBROSE
 What'll we hitch it to?

KEATING
 That's the least of our worries.

AMBROSE
 See if you can plop him back into the cot, Wing. Cot!
 Don't let him bite you. Bite! Don't let him.

 WING sort of understands.

KEATING
 I never would have thought of building a railroad up
 through there, you know. I have to hand it to the
 Major. The moon. That's using your noggin.

AMBROSE
 It's what makes him such an exceptional bloody
 genius.

KEATING
 Surveying the lunar surface won't be easy, though.

AMBROSE
 No.

KEATING

All those naked women running around. I hope you
won't find it too uncomfortable. I know how you are
about all that. Leave me alone, you. What are you
doing?

AMBROSE

He's trying to get you back up into your cot.

KEATING

Why?

AMBROSE

Because you've fallen out of it, stupid.

WING

Ho fan ah.

KEATING

(*to WING, as WING gets him into the cot*) You're not such
a bad egg, you know; after all is said and blah-de-blah.
You have your faults, yes, I'll be the first to admit it.
But you try hard. And apart from smelling vaguely
like a piece of rotting flesh –

AMBROSE

That *is* rotting flesh.

KEATING

– you're alright.

AMBROSE

It's got to come off, this.

KEATING

I'd like to take this opportunity to thank you and to
thank everyone for all their good work. This hasn't
been just fun and games, you know. Ambrose here
got a bit of gangrene, and I had quite, quite itchy
cobblers at one point.

He has a seizure. WING recoils.

AMBROSE

> Stand back. He's having another one of his attacks.
> Bring that knife over here. I'll do this myself. Wing.
> Over here! Never mind him. He'll calm down in a
> minute.
>
> > *The seizure subsides, and KEATING falls unconscious again.*
>
> Here. Give me that thing.

WING

> Ding nei gor fei.

AMBROSE

> Don't be stupid. It's got to come off. Give it.
>
> > *With shaky hand, WING offers the knife to AMBROSE.*
>
> Oh, for God's sake. It's just a leg. Right, then.
>
> > *An enormous intake of breath, knife in hand, throws his
> > arm back.*
>
> I can't do it! I can't do it!
>
> > *Beat.*
>
> Yes I can!
>
> > *He stabs down on his leg; digs in with all his might;
> > shivering and weeping with revulsion. He passes out.
> > WING stands, looking at both men.*

WING

> Gow meng ah.
>
> > *Blackout.*

Scene Seven

Now in a greatly advanced state of pain, a knife stuck in his leg, AMBROSE tries to write in his journal. KEATING is having some small convulsions. Eventually they stop. KEATING wakes.

KEATING
I've had the most bizarre dream. I was an actor in a dreadful play that wouldn't end. I was playing a stupid git who had rabies. I didn't know any of my lines, so whenever it was my turn to speak I would have convulsions. You were in the dream. I had to blabber on insanely about hitching a rope to the moon. The audience was completely stupefied, so in a fit of nervousness, I pretended to pass out.

AMBROSE
Really.

KEATING
I've been thinking.

AMBROSE
Have you?

KEATING
I have. You know – I'm quite looking forward, you know, to getting back to the coast. Seeing Melinda again. Sticking my head between her tits and blowing with my lips and all that. What about you?

AMBROSE

    I hardly know her.

KEATING

    You know what I mean.

AMBROSE

    I'm feeling a little circumspect about the whole thing, at this point.

KEATING

    I wonder why I can't move.

AMBROSE

    Move or not move; does it really matter?

KEATING

    What are you doing?

AMBROSE

    Making a last entry into my journal.

KEATING

    It's about time you gave that up. What's the point of a journal, I want to know.

AMBROSE

    Perhaps it'll serve as a warning. A cautionary tale of men trying to reach further than they ought.

KEATING

    Well, you see; I don't believe in that.

AMBROSE

    I know you don't. That's the point.

KEATING

    Shall I tell you what I believe? Alright. I believe – what do I believe? I believe that, that – that – I'm not sure, actually. Yes, I am. I believe – I believe – that men –

all men – including women – all of us, I believe –
believe – well, that's it, really. I believe.

AMBROSE

In what?

KEATING

Oh, well. That's a – that's a – I'm sorry. What were we
talking about?

AMBROSE

We were talking about men and railroads, and folly.

KEATING

Were we?

AMBROSE

I was.

KEATING

And what was I talking about?

AMBROSE

I have no idea.

KEATING

Folly?

AMBROSE

Human enterprise. The great stretch of man's
imagination. What's it all for? A railroad. To what?
From what? It's not just that. It's the whole catalogue
of human achievement; you can dump it all in a big
pile of rubble as far as I'm concerned, because in the
end, it still comes back to this. Flesh, rotting.

KEATING

Do us a favour. Don't ever go into the songwriting
business.

AMBROSE
> People need to know the truth.

KEATING
> That's not the truth. The truth is – what's the truth?
> I know. The truth is that God is looking down on
> each and every one of us – and he's saying, "If you
> want to get to heaven, you'd bloody well better map
> it out and build a pathway through those mountains,
> because on the other side – on the other side, are
> the pearly gates."

AMBROSE
> Do you know what you're talking about?

KEATING
> No, but I like the sound of it.

AMBROSE
> We're not going back to the coast.

KEATING
> Of course we are.

AMBROSE
> Your faith will finally let you down. At least that's
> something to be grateful for. There's no one coming,
> you're dying, and we're in the middle of nowhere.
> That's it. In other words, even if you weren't done for,
> you'd be damned.

KEATING
> But I have a way out.

> *As AMBROSE speaks, KEATING dies.*

AMBROSE
> A way out? Madness; is that it? There's no way out.
> What have we left, Keating? The Major and his men

marching over the mountain? It's as unlikely as it is alliterative.

WING enters, goes to KEATING.

It's over. We should never have come.

WING
Zhwai gin.

He covers KEATING over with a blanket.

AMBROSE
What is it? Is he dead? Lucky bastard.

Beat.

Get the gun. Gun! Let's just end it. What have I left? Besides you. Nothing. A Wing, and a prayer; that's it. Not even a prayer.

Blackout.

Scene Eight

KEATING is gone. WING is trying to spoon soup into AMBROSE. He won't take it. WING holds his head, wiping his brow.

AMBROSE

I hope you appreciate what I've done here, Wing. I've left you that bullet. There. See? You've an option, now. Protect yourself, or do yourself in. Bit of a philosophical dilemma, really. It's the least I could do for you and anyway, never mind about me. It'll be over soon enough for me. I can already hear the strains of "Rock of Ages" as sung by the straw-bonnetted bovines in the ladies' auxiliary. Speech by my father to follow, peppered with the usual hypocrisies. Then off to shag his mistress. Thank God I'll be dead.

WING

Yam tsa.

AMBROSE

Don't want anything, thanks.

Neither says anything for a moment, as AMBROSE is cradled by WING. WING begins to cry.

What are you doing? Stop crying, for God's sake. I'd prefer not to be the source of anyone's tears at this point. You don't even know me. This is embarrassing. Get a grip, man. Listen to me; I want you to give this to the first person that comes along. If nobody comes along, I want you to bury it in that metal box over there. It's a journal. It contains some of the worst prose ever written. I want the world to know what this country can do to a man's writing style. But more importantly, I want there to be – I want there to be something left of me on this earth that matters. Something ... left.

He begins to cry along with WING. They cry together.

Or perhaps not. Perhaps it's fitting to end it this way; no one knowing, much less caring. Who are we to be remembered? Eh, Wing? Who are we?

WING speaks the following in Chinese, here translated into English for the information of the reader.

WING

Ngo mmm ming bat lay.
(*I don't understand you.*)

AMBROSE

Charters of territories; drawers of lines? Who are we? There is no land; only ground to wander, and earth to be – buried ... in ...

WING

Ngo jun hai hoe sui uh.
(*I feel just terrible.*)

Ngo lum ngo joe joh geen hoe cho ga see.
(*I think I made a terrible mistake.*)

Hay lo ying go die yut man, ngo lay yuen geen do yow dee yun.
(*The first night we camped here, I saw some men far in the distance.*)

Ngo hoe gang, so yee ngo jing sick dee foa-hay mong go dee yun wun mmm do ngo day.
(*Because I was scared, I put out the fire, so they wouldn't find us.*)

Gun ju lay goa leung man la, ngo jung hai hoe gang, gum ngo how jue lay day fun joa jee how, joi jing sick dee foa.
(*For the next two nights, because I was so scared, I put out the fire when you were asleep.*)

Dun hae yee ga, ngo lum, go dee yun hai seung lay bong ngo day ga.
(*But now I think that we were supposed to meet up with them.*)

Ngo lum kui day hai ying goi lai wun ngo day ga.
(*I think they were supposed to find us.*)

Chuen boh do hai ngo ga choa.
(*It's all my fault.*)

Ngo yee ga mut yeah do lum mmm doe.
(*Now I don't know what to think.*)

Mmmm jee ngo day wui deem?
(*What will happen?*)

Ngo mmm seung hai doe.
(*I don't want to be here.*)

Ngo mmm seung loaw hai dee go san guk.
(*I don't want to be in this valley.*)

Ngo mmm seung hai dee go gock ga.
(*I don't want to be in this country.*)

Ngo jung dee goa gock ga.
(*I hate this country.*)

Lee doe moe yun jung yee ngo ga, yow mo yun ming bak ngo.
(*Nobody likes me here, nobody understands me here.*)

Ngo do mmm jee doe ngo yee ga hai been doe.
(*And now I don't know where I am.*)

Ngo seung fan ook kay uh. Ngo jing hai seung seung fan ook kay jah.
(*I just want to go home. I want to go home.*)

> *AMBROSE has died. WING gently lets his head down, then covers him, too, with a blanket. Both men dead, WING sits in the middle of the tent, as the wind picks up.*

WING
Ngo seung fan ook kay uh. Ngo jing hai seung seung fan ook kay jah.
(*I just want to go home. I want to go home.*)

> *Lights slowly fade on the scene. Blackout.*

> *The End.*